KEEPING KIDS SAFE

in a

DIGITAL WORLD

A Solution That Works

MANDY MAJORS

To my three favorite people—
Thanks for letting me share some of our stories.
Always know I love you, no matter what.

TABLE OF CONTENTS

INTRODUCTION

"Wake up!" I shouted as I raced down the hallway to my daughter's room. "We can't be late for school again!"

Rushing into her closet, I frantically rummaged through purple and teal hangers to find something for her to wear. *Is it warm enough for shorts? Jeans?*

From the bedroom, I heard a meek little voice. My sweet girl asked a question I wasn't prepared for. I froze right there in her closet.

At that moment, I would've given anything for the "Where do babies come from?" question.

I was stunned. Her question was highly sexualized—and detailed. I didn't even know this "thing" she was asking about existed until I was a nineteen-year-old college student. And she was only NINE!

My thoughts spiraled. *Why is my fourth grader asking me a question like this? What has she been exposed to that she would know something this detailed?* I felt like my daughter's innocence had been stolen.

After collecting myself, I stepped out of the closet and walked over to her bed. I could feel my heart pounding as I sat down next to her.

"Thank you so much for asking me," I said calmly as I looked her in the eyes. "That's what I want you to do when you're curious. But we're going to be late for school, so can we talk about this later?"

That bought me some time.

That afternoon, while my daughter was doing homework at our kitchen island, I initiated a conversation about the question she had asked. Eventually I discovered that another nine-year-old child had watched a sexually graphic online video at home and then shared the details with a group of fourth graders. No screens were present, but my child had clearly been exposed to pornography.

That was the moment I realized parenting had changed.

I would love to tell you that I handled the situation with grace, but the truth is, I was angry and bitter for weeks. Many nights, after my husband and I prayed with our kids before bedtime, we'd rant and rave behind closed doors in our bedroom.

"What is happening to our society?"

"Do these crazy parents know what their kids are telling other children?"

"Kids today are growing up way too fast!"

We even talked about moving to a remote island where we could live "off the grid." Sounds nice, right?

What happened to our baby girl was like a slap in the face, and I wasn't sure what to do. I felt like we had been responsible parents by not giving her a phone. We thought we were protecting her, but she was still exposed to pornography.

In a knee-jerk response, my husband and I said no to *all* technology. We were only trying to keep our child safe, but she felt like we were punishing her. Our good intentions ultimately led to a breakdown in our relationship.

Months later, my husband and I were lying in bed one night, totally depleted. As we prayed together, he suddenly reached for my hand and said, "Instead of saying no to all technology, let's teach ourselves how to parent it."

I immediately sat up and said, "Yes! Our kids need to know how to navigate the online world safely. But how do we teach them to do that?"

"I have no idea," he confessed.

So we embarked on a journey to figure it out. That was seven years ago, and I've been on a mission to keep kids safe ever since.

I eventually shared our story with the women's pastor at our church, and she encouraged me to start a moms' group. Approximately twenty women came to that first meeting, and the group quickly grew to around two hundred moms. Soon we exceeded our childcare budget and even had people wait-listed to join our group. At that point, one of the pastors encouraged us to make our resources available outside the church, because every parent needed this information.

So in 2016, we formed nextTalk, a 501(c)(3) organization in the state of Texas. The founding families in our nonprofit had kids from two to twenty years of age in private and public schools, as well as homeschool. Different educational settings work for different families, but we saw the same problems in all three environments because the online world is *everywhere*.

In February 2017, I published my first book, *TALK: A Practical Approach to Cyberparenting and Open Communication*. Then in May of that year, nextTalk launched a radio program on a local station in San Antonio and recorded a new show every week. We started out with just a few hundred listeners, and in just three years, our podcast audience expanded to tens of thousands in sixty countries. It has been incredible to watch God grow our organization!

In 2018, we produced a nine-week video study titled *Where Do I Start?* Each thirty-minute video features moms, dads, and kids and includes discussion questions. To date, our videos have been viewed in thirty-seven states and twenty countries.

In 2019, *TALK* won first place in the Family/Parenting category of the Illumination Book Awards. Since then, I've shared my story with thousands of people as I've traveled across Texas, Ohio, Virginia, Kentucky, Pennsylvania, and Georgia. Only God!

I love meeting families and spending one-on-one time with parents at our nextTalk events. I've learned so much from them, and their stories have deeply impacted my passion to keep kids safe online.

I started this book in early 2020, but then the COVID pandemic hit. Before I knew it, our lives turned upside down.

Lockdowns and social distancing kicked in, our nextTalk events were postponed, and kids began using technology even more for school, church, socializing, everything. In spite of all the chaos, we kept recording a new weekly podcast, and I focused on completing this writing project.

I've written this book, in part, because so many people have asked for a resource that summarizes my event presentations. I also recognize that parents are busy, so I've zeroed in on the most relevant issues we're dealing with today. If you've read *TALK*, you'll find that I've added some new stories and ideas in this book. The heart of my message hasn't changed (you'll see this similarity between the two books), but I wanted to share some of the new things I've been learning.

If you need a quick-reference guide, this little book is your go-to source. But I also encourage you to dig into *TALK* for more detailed information on the issues we cover in this book, as well as additional topics and background. These books are designed to complement each other.

In the chapters that follow, we'll first identify the problem we're facing as parents in today's digital world. We've been blindsided by the new parenting challenges technology has created, and we suddenly realize that we're in uncharted territory. As parents, we often say things like "Technology is changing how kids are growing up," but what does that really mean? We'll dive into those details in chapter 1.

Then I'll take you along on my search for answers to the problem and share the solution I discovered that really works. My grasp of how to implement this solution has deepened in so many ways since I wrote *TALK*.

Finally we'll wrap up with ten practical ideas for implementing the solution. (This is my favorite part!) Along the way, I'll share specific examples of how Old Mandy used to respond to parenting issues and how New Mandy responds now. I want you to clearly see how my parenting approach has changed.

As you read this book, my hope is that you'll not only see yourself in the stories but come away with some helpful ideas you can implement in your own home.

1

IDENTIFYING THE PROBLEM

Last year I was speaking at a conference about the new problem we're facing as parents. I was in the middle of sharing a story about what technology is exposing our kids to, when a mama walked out … hyperventilating.

The last thing I want to do is make you hyperventilate! I struggle with how much to tell you because I don't want to scare you. But I also know that we can't parent effectively if we don't understand the problem or see it clearly. We can't protect our children from danger if we're clueless about what's happening in their world.

So let's bring the problem into the light and examine it with eyes wide open.

What is this new problem? *Technology is exposing our kids to dangers and adult issues they're not equipped to handle.*

The explosive growth of technology means that kids today are connecting to the world at younger ages than ever before. What they're encountering online not only exposes them to danger, but it also raises complicated questions and issues that many parents (including me!) feel inadequate to address. I mean, how do you talk to a fourth grader about porn?

In this chapter, we're going to break down some of the parenting issues we face so we can better understand the shift that has taken place because of technology. For this discussion, I've chosen issues I've encountered firsthand or hear most often from parents.

First, we'll look at new things we have to parent that no other generation has had to deal with before: social media, YouTube, apps, screen addiction, and nudes. Then we'll dive into issues that have been around for years but have shifted because of technology: strangers and sex trafficking, pornography, sexuality and transgender, cutting, bullying, and suicide.

We're going to move pretty fast, so buckle up!

Social Media

Most of us can't call our parents and say, "How did you handle Snapchat?"

They're like "Snap what?"

We're the first generation to parent social media. Normally we teach our kids how to do things. But with social media, they're actually teaching us.

As parents, we know that social media is about connection, likes, and followers, but we don't always realize that it exposes children to all kinds of potentially harmful influences as well. Think about rejection for a moment. Because of social media, kids know when they're not invited to a party. And if your child is struggling to find her own friend group (as most kids do), she is constantly reminded that she doesn't have one whenever she goes on social media and sees pictures of her peers with their own best friends.

Let's take this one step further.

If your child doesn't make the basketball team and then sees posts of team friendships and the championship win five months later, it's a continual jab that reminds him, "You weren't good enough for that group."

When I was growing up, rejection might sting for a week or so. But now it's constantly in our kids' faces whenever they scroll through social media.

Trending hashtags are another way social media is changing our culture. One example is the expression "Love is love." Sounds sweet, right? When kids see this sentiment trending, it can become engrained as a foundational truth that applies to every situation. But does it apply to a twelve-year-old girl who believes she's in love and wants to run away with a sixty-five-year-old man she met on Instagram?

It might be trending, but is it truth?

Most popular hashtags and expressions are cute sentiments, but they can't be applied to every situation. Do you see how social media can distort what's true and even put our kids in dangerous situations?

Because of the reach of social media, kids are also afraid of being canceled. Cancel culture is a pile-on mob mentality where people try to ruin someone's reputation, college acceptance, career, you name it. My sixteen-year-old explained to me that it's more toxic than disagreeing with people or calling them out for inappropriate or inexcusable behavior; it's about ruining their lives. Some comments even take it to the extreme of telling kids to kill themselves or making them wish they were dead. Cancel culture is bullying, which I'll expand on in a moment.

Social media is a complex issue, the effects of which we'll be dissecting for many years to come.

In my book *TALK*, you can read about other aspects of social media that our kids encounter on a regular basis, including popularity, comparisons, and desensitization.

Next, we'll look at another new parenting issue that intertwines with social media.

YouTube

Do you remember the Tide Pod Challenge? Kids were actually eating pods filled with laundry detergent! When that social media challenge went viral, people were posting memes and comments online, asking, "How can kids be so stupid?"

Comments like that tell me we don't understand our kids' culture. Let me explain.

As adults, what do we do when the washer breaks down and we don't want to spend eight hundred dollars for a repair visit? We YouTube it! We watch someone else demonstrate the repair on a screen, and then we imitate the behavior.

What do our kids do if they want to learn a new skill like riding a bike, skateboarding, or applying makeup? They YouTube it.

So why in the world should we be surprised when they watch someone eating Tide Pods on their screens and then imitate that behavior?

We're not raising stupid kids. They are geniuses and know how to do more with technology than we ever will. They're just doing what their culture is telling them to do. Watch the screen; imitate the behavior.

If we don't understand their culture, we miss this entirely. But when we see it clearly, we recognize there is a step kids need to take before imitating the behavior. To parent an issue effectively, we must see it first.

Kids also want validation, so when they watch and imitate their favorite YouTuber, they often think they'll be seen and heard too. Many children even dream of becoming the next YouTube star. Influencers who have built a large platform of followers get paid serious money to advertise products on their channels and social media platforms. It's appealing to kids that they could make cash for having followers while getting the validation they crave.

How else does YouTube impact our culture? When I was growing up, almost everyone loved the same actor from the most popular TV show at the time. But today there are so many streaming platforms, you probably don't even know the name of your child's favorite YouTuber. Right? I can't keep up.

On top of that, our kids often develop a personal connection with their YouTubers and think of them as friends. Compared to the actors we loved growing up, YouTubers post details about their everyday lives as they unfold. Using their platforms, they'll typically record from their homes with their "significant other" and their pets. Making personal connections with their viewers means that YouTubers have even more input and influence in our children's lives. In a way, YouTubers have become another kind of educator in our kids' world.

YouTube stars whom our kids feel they know personally have an impact on their worldview, shaping their views on politics, religion, sexuality, transgender, and so much more. YouTubers have our kids' attention, so we need to be aware of how they're influencing and educating them.

Apps

Apps today are constantly changing. That's something our parents never had to keep up with.

A couple of years into learning how to cyberparent, I implemented an app-approval system with my kids. If they asked for a new game, for example, we'd play it together first. If it appeared safe, I'd approve the app.

My son, who was nine at the time, asked if he could download a bunny app that had a 9-plus rating. (FYI: I have two kids. My son is now thirteen, and my daughter is sixteen.)

I played the game with him and concluded the content was fine. To earn tokens, he had to clean up the bunny's "poop." (I have no idea why that was fun, but he loved this crazy app!) After making sure there was no chat feature or connection to strangers, I gave my approval. I thought I was doing all the right things.

Weeks later, as I was folding laundry, I heard my son screaming in the kitchen. When I raced into the room, I found him sitting at the island with the family iPad.

He urgently explained, "Mom, I'm playing the bunny-app game. At the bottom it said, 'Click here for more tokens,' and I need those tokens to buy more items in the store. So I clicked it, and this popped up."

He turned the screen toward me, and I couldn't believe what I saw. (Brace yourself!) In a cartoon-like scene, two naked men were lying in bed together, and a girl was standing over them. A talk bubble above the girl said, "You're *cheating* on me?!" The bubbles below showed two choices: "Run away crying!" or "Join them!"

FOR A THREESOME! My nine-year-old son had been exposed to a *threesome* on an app I had vetted and approved. (To see the screenshots, go to my website, mandymajors.com, and type "bunny" in the search window.)

Since then, I've done a lot of research on this issue, but I can't find any requirements that pop-up ads must match an app's age rating. So our kids can be innocently playing a 9-plus-rated app and be exposed to pop-up ads that don't match that rating. Even if laws are updated to address this, there will always be loopholes with technology.

Apps change daily. How do we keep up with it all to protect our kids from adult content?

Screen Addiction

As parents, we've always had to worry about our children becoming addicted to drugs or alcohol. It's still a huge concern as kids try to find an escape from mounting pressures. But now we're facing a new parenting challenge: screen addiction.

When we were little, we didn't have the option of gaming all day or going live from our bedrooms to tell the world our feelings. Screens have not only given our children more options for how to spend their time, but they've also increased the risk of addiction.

Did you know that screen addiction is one of the top reasons for poor academic performance in school, as well as dropping out of college?[1] A growing number of kids are addicted to technology by the time they enter college. They can't even regulate their screen time without their parents telling them, "Your screen time is up!"

Technology addictions are real, and the withdrawal symptoms are too. In fact, Dr. Richard Graham, who opened a technology addiction program in the United Kingdom in 2010 (that's TEN years ago!), found that "young technology addicts experienced the same withdrawal symptoms as alcoholics or heroin addicts when [their] devices were taken away."[2] These symptoms may include irritability, temper tantrums, depression, and even violence. (For more information on screen and gaming addictions, see the "Addictions" chapter in my book *TALK*.)

Have you ever watched the controller fly across the room after telling your child to turn off the Xbox?

Have you seen your child curled up in a ball on the couch in a daze, scrolling through social media for hours?

How do you react when your spouse says, "Can you please get off Facebook?"

(I struggle with all of the above.)

You guys, how can we help our kids find a healthy balance with screens if we aren't living this out ourselves?

We're the first generation of parents who have to figure out how to regulate screen time and protect our kids from becoming addicted to technology. At the same time, we need to be careful not to overreact. Kids are using screens now more than ever (especially with all the virtual learning taking place as I write this book), so it can be easy to overindulge in screen time. But there's a big difference between overindulgence and addiction. As parents, we need to beware of the red flags that lead to addiction, but let's make sure we don't water down the importance of that term by overusing it.

Nudes

Another dangerous trend with kids is sharing nude photos (nudes, for short). According to one survey, "[Sixty-six percent] of teens and young adults ... have received a sexually explicit image and 41% have sent one."[3]

I've helped some really good parents deal with their children sharing nudes. First, I encourage parents to just love their kids and show grace, no matter what. Then once we start talking through the issue, I'll ask if they've ever discussed nudes with their children. Almost always, their response is "I didn't know I had to." That tells me once again that we really don't understand our kids' culture. They are growing up in a different world, where nudes have been normalized.

We tend to think that girls are the only ones who send nude photos. But that isn't the case. Boys also send nudes called *dick pics*. (Don't cringe. You need to know this.) In some geographical locations, sharing nudes is referred to as *trading cards*. You know, like how we used to trade baseball cards.

The mainstream media often refers to this trend as *sexting*—a combination of the words *sex* and *text*. I think that term is outdated. It's also misleading for parents because kids don't really sext anymore. They share nudes within apps because it's easier to hide the pictures and more difficult to track.

People have shared stories with me about eighth-grade girls saying, "If you haven't been asked for a nude by now, you're kinda lame."

Did you catch that?

Our world is telling our baby girls that they should *want* to be asked for a nude because it validates their beauty, popularity, and desirability. Kids crave validation, and being asked for a nude tells a girl she's good enough.

What is happening?

These are just a few of the most challenging *new* issues we face today. Next, we'll look at some parenting issues that have been around for years but have significantly changed because of technology.

Strangers and Sex Traffickers

When I was growing up, kids were warned about stranger danger. I remember my mom saying, "Don't get in the white van with the guy offering you candy." Anyone else?

I'm not talking about nice white vans. I'm talking about the old painter kind with fabric-covered windows, or no windows at all. (I have no idea why white vans get picked on, but you get my point, right?)

In today's world, we still have to be concerned about stranger danger and our children being kidnapped. Absolutely! But technology has made the issue even more complicated. Online strangers, including sex traffickers, now have access to our kids through social media, apps, and gaming systems. Your eleven-year-old can be sitting next to you on the family sofa chatting with another kid online. But behind the profile picture of a young boy could actually be a sex-trafficking pimp.

Online sex traffickers can reach our children in our homes, at school, at a friend's house—anywhere. Traffickers often act as if they're the same age as the child they're chatting with. To establish a personal connection, they identify with a child's feelings and experiences, like messaging, "I hate my parents!" To groom a child, a sex trafficker might exchange private messages on social media or through an app and try to get the child to do something bad. When the child does, the sex trafficker might say something like "If you don't send me a nude, I'll send these messages to your mom on Facebook."

A child who is blackmailed into sending a nude can be blackmailed into doing just about anything. For example, a sex trafficker might say to your child, "Go to this app, take off your clothes, and livestream from 8:00 to 10:00 p.m." When your child complies, the pimp collects money from porn viewers as your kid is sex-trafficked in his or her own bedroom!

The digital world has given sex traffickers unprecedented access to our children, and that access enables them to build relationships with our kids that can lead to grooming and sex trafficking.

One more thought on this subject before we move on. It was recently brought to my attention that a teenage girl was persuaded to take photos of her feet and send them to an online stranger, who paid a lot of money for the pictures. The girl didn't think it was wrong because it wasn't a nude. Have your guard up! This is a gateway to more trafficking. Teens are cashing in on schemes like this, and if there's good money in it, they can easily be enticed into this dark world.

I know this is tough to hear, but hang with me. Do you see why we have to understand our kids' culture if we're going to parent these issues effectively?

Pornography

Pornography has always been around, but it has changed in two significant ways: (1) Technology has made porn incredibly easy to access anytime, anywhere; and (2) the type of pornography available online today is different from the porn that existed when we were kids.

First, let's talk about access. When we were growing up, it would take a covert operation for young boys to get their hands on a porn magazine with naked girls. I don't mean to be sexist, but that's basically what happened. If a boy actually got his hands on a porn magazine, he had to hide the forbidden contraband under a mattress or in the back of a closet. Some video stores even had private rooms in the back, but access was restricted to adults with a photo ID. Do y'all remember that? I distinctly recall being introduced to those backroom videos in college.

Today your young kids can be curled up next to you in a corner of the family sectional with earbuds in place and their small screens hidden from view ... watching porn videos.

Another way porn has changed is that a growing number of girls are watching it. I've noticed this trend through the stories I hear. It's not just a boy thing anymore.

At nextTalk, the issue parents contact us about most often is their kids' exposure to pornography. The youngest child exposed to porn that we've been contacted about so far was five years old. Exposure is happening with younger children because pornography is more accessible than ever. And since it's readily available, it isn't taboo anymore. Kids aren't always shocked by pornography, so it's not unusual for them to casually talk about it with their friends.

In addition to access, pornography has changed in another significant way: The type of pornography our kids are watching is different from the porn that existed when we were kids. Girls have always been objectified in pornography, but now boys are victims too.

Do you know that in 2019, one of the most common search terms on Pornhub was *anal sex*?[4] Anal sex not only objectifies boys in male-male porn, but it's becoming popular in girl-guy teen relationships because there is no pregnancy risk. It's an issue no one talks about. Other popular search terms were *lesbian*, *threesome*, and *stepmom*. (By the way, if you see kids referencing "Ph," that stands for *Pornhub*.)

Children today are watching pornography that features two males, two females, threesomes—you get the picture. When an elementary-age child is exposed to these types of videos, it can trigger a normal biological response. But if the child hasn't had any healthy conversations about sex, this can lead to confusion.

Our nextTalk team is hearing more of these stories from parents at our events across the country. When one child came out to her mom as lesbian, her mom loved her unconditionally, as we always recommend. I encouraged this mom to press into conversations with her daughter to figure out the *why* behind this revelation. After several weeks, she discovered that her child had been watching pornography. Her daughter said she preferred watching female-female pornography because the male-female porn always hurt the female. The male was always the aggressor. But the porn with two females was gentler. There was no way this child ever wanted to be in a relationship with a boy because she assumed that a real relationship looks like that rough male-female porn.

I'm not saying that all kids who question their sexuality have been exposed to pornography. No. But pornography can cause our kids to be confused about their sexuality. I see this happen often and hear stories about it from parents.

At one nextTalk event, a mom shared with me privately that her son had been sexually abused many years ago. The abuser was an eleven-year-old cousin who showed her son a pornographic video and said, "Do this to me." At the time of the abuse, her son was five. There was only one wall separating this mom from her child at a family gathering when the abuse took place.

I still remember the look on her face and the sadness in her eyes. Pornography fuels abuse.

I could share more stories about kids using pornography to sexually abuse other kids. People around us are living this nightmare—even those "good" families who sit next to us in church and look like they have it all together. Most of them are suffering in silence because they're afraid of being judged.

Let me add another layer to this discussion. One of our next-Talk volunteers, who has worked with kids for almost twenty years as a public-school teacher and an assistant principal, shared this sobering observation: "Pornography used to be a pinup supermodel you'd never meet. Today it's the girl sitting next to you in math class."

Think about that for a minute. A twelve-year-old boy is sitting next to a girl who shared her nude photo last night with her boyfriend. Then her boyfriend air-dropped it to the entire football team. This is our kids' world. Imagine trying to process this as a child.

We have to protect our children from this danger! It's not only about shielding them from a sexually explicit picture or video; it's about guarding their hearts and minds from the life-altering damage and destruction that the dark web of pornography causes. It creates confusion about sexuality, it fuels abuse, it treats people as objects, and it increases the demand for sex trafficking. There's a reason pimps try to get our kids to take their clothes off and livestream from their bedrooms. Pornography pays.

At this point you might be thinking, *Why am I reading this? I'll never sleep again!*

Stay with me.

Remember what I said earlier? We can't parent the issues effectively if we don't understand our kids' culture. We MUST know what they're facing. If we see the problem for what it is, we can actively work toward a solution. Our kids are worth it!

Sexuality and Transgender

Sexuality isn't a new parenting issue, but technology has given our children unprecedented access to sexual content online. What kids see or hear often leads to confusion, especially for young children, and it raises questions that can be difficult for parents to answer.

One morning on the drive to school, my eleven-year-old asked, "What does bisexual mean?"

Once again, my child asked a question that caught me off guard. Then my sixth grader proceeded to tell me that a lot of girls at school said they were "bi."

I knew this was going to require a lengthy conversation, so I replied, "That's a really important question. Can we talk about it when we have more time? I promise I won't forget." Then I said, "If someone is being disrespectful or making fun of a child who identifies as bisexual, speak up. Be kind to everyone and never bully or make fun of anyone. And always stand up for others. Be nice. Be a light." (We'll come back to that conversation later in the book.)

Kids today hear terms like *bisexual* and *transgender* on social media or from their peers without understanding what they mean. At the same time, they feel enormous pressure to label themselves and check a box. Puberty is confusing enough for kids, but technology is making their lives even more complicated. This is another area of parenting that has shifted.

Let's talk about transgender for a minute. Sexuality and transgender are both complex topics, but they're very different. Sexuality deals with sexual attraction and sexual acts, while transgender is about gender identity and perception. (I'd encourage you to read the chapters on sexuality and transgender in my book *TALK* or listen to our nextTalk podcasts for a more in-depth discussion.)

When my son was in third grade, a debate was trending online about a transgender wrestler. Kids were actually arguing about it on the school playground at recess! My son had questions. Your kids do too. Technology has radically changed the things our kids think about and the questions they ask, so our parenting approach has to change as well. We're in new territory!

Cutting

Every day my kids and I pray in the car on the way to school. One morning, when my daughter was in seventh grade, there was a long pause during her prayer.

When I asked, "What's wrong?" she hesitated and then replied, "I know girls personally in all seven of my classes who are cutting."

Cutting is a form of self-harming. Boys and girls who self-harm not only cut themselves, but they may also pull out their hair, burn themselves, or hurt themselves in other ways.

Self-harming has been around for a while, but this is another trend that has accelerated with social media. Some kids even post online about their cutting experiences.

When I first heard about cutting, I thought it was like a suicide attempt because my mind went to slit wrists. But I quickly learned from talking with a number of counselors that this often isn't the case. Kids typically self-harm because the physical pain is a release for their emotional pain.

Kids today are stressed and overwhelmed. A lot of information is coming at them fast, and when they don't know how to process their emotions, self-harming can become an unhealthy coping strategy. If this strategy stops working, however, they may search for other destructive ways to cope with their pain, or they may even spiral toward suicide.

According to the Mayo Clinic, "Although self-injury is not usually a suicide attempt, it can increase the risk of suicide because of the emotional problems that trigger self-injury. And the pattern of damaging the body in times of distress can make suicide more likely."[5]

Always take self-harm seriously. It's a red flag that something is going on emotionally that your child isn't able to express or deal with. If your child is self-harming, talk with a health-care professional who understands the problem and can help you and your child address the underlying issues.

A licensed professional counselor who volunteers with next-Talk also offers this advice: "Parents should always seek out professional counseling to rule out past trauma or unreported/unhealed sexual abuse or assault. Kids who cut have often experienced non-consensual crossing of boundaries by someone they know."

Above all, love your child and press into conversations to find out *why* he or she is cutting. *What inside turmoil is your child trying to escape from?* Your baby is trying to numb the pain that he or she may not be able to communicate in words. If you don't address the issue now, it could evolve into a bigger problem, such as drug use, sexual promiscuity, or even suicide.

Bullying

Bullying has been around forever. I remember kids getting picked on and made fun of when I was in school. But technology has magnified the problem—especially social media, where kids can easily snap a photo, create a meme, or post a video.

Picture your sixth-grade boy, who isn't allowed on social media. An eighth grader at school is bullying him, and a circle of kids gather around to watch.

What happens next? Something that didn't happen when we were kids.

Phones come out, and everyone starts recording the incident. If your little boy cries or turns red, phones are in his face, capturing every embarrassing detail in real time. Before he walks out of the building, those videos have been Snapchatted to the entire school population, and memes making fun of your child are being posted to anonymous accounts.

Even though your child isn't on social media, he's humiliated, and his thoughts are spiraling about what's circulating online and maybe even going viral.

When he comes home at the end of the day, he tells you, "My life is over. I can't go back to school."

How do we typically respond as parents?

"Oh, it can't be *that* bad. Will anyone remember next year? Every kid has been humiliated at some point in front of other kids. Toughen up!"

I'm guilty.

You know what? This response shows me yet again that we don't understand our kids' world. Those videos could actually follow your child when he applies to college or interviews for his first job. We didn't have that kind of fear when we were kids.

Cyberbullying never stops. It's 24/7. And the harassment and humiliation spread faster because of technology.

Why is this important? Because kids who are cyberbullied are two times more likely to commit suicide.[6]

To protect our kids, we must recognize this shift.

Suicide

I can't imagine anything more devastating for a parent than losing a child. On this journey, I've crossed paths with parents who have lost their kids to suicide, and let me tell you, there are no words in these kinds of situations. Only tears.

Suicide happens in good families with good parents. So please don't ever think it can't happen in your home to your own child. No family is immune.

If your child is suicidal, reach out to a medical doctor and a licensed counselor, and always, always take suicide threats seriously. Remember: our kids need our unconditional love and support no matter what they're going through.

Did you know that suicide is the *second* leading cause of death for kids between the ages of ten and twenty-four?[7]

Ten years old. That's fourth grade!

We have a problem.

More children are committing suicide today, but why? It's complicated, and many factors contribute to the problem.

When I was writing my first book, suicide was the last issue I needed to research. I remember sitting in my office thinking, *Do I even need to research this? After seeing this big scary picture come together, I get it. Kids are dealing with so much. They are processing pornography, possibly questioning their sexuality, being asked for nudes, sorting through social media, struggling with screen addiction, constantly afraid of being bullied and recorded, and may be trying to numb the pain and pressure of it all by self-harming or using mind-altering substances. At the same time, parents don't realize how the world has changed. We don't get it. If our kids try to talk to us, we often don't know what to say. It's the perfect storm that leaves our kids feeling trapped, isolated, and alone.*

It's difficult to talk about suicide, but we need to bring it out of the shadows for the sake of our kids. We are literally fighting for their lives.

John 10:10 warns us that Satan comes "to steal, kill and destroy" our families. He is "like a lion prowling around looking for an opportunity to devour" our kids (1 Peter 5:8).

I know you may feel completely overwhelmed after reading this chapter, but hope and help are on the way. I promise.

2

SEARCHING FOR A SOLUTION THAT WORKS

At first, all I could see was this big scary problem of parenting kids in a digital world. My nine-year-old daughter didn't have a phone, and yet she had been exposed to pornography. After hearing horrific stories from other parents, all I wanted to do was protect her.

My gut response to the problem was no phones, no technology—EVER! It seemed like the right solution at the time, so my husband and I made this our new family rule.

But guess what happened when we bubble-wrapped our child and tried to control her every move. A wall went up between us, and communication shut down. Our daughter felt more and more like we didn't understand her world. She was right.

Bubble-wrapping didn't solve the problem; it only damaged our relationship. There had to be another way.

In this chapter, I'll walk you through my trial-and-error search for a solution. That search ultimately led to a life-transforming discovery that changed my approach to parenting—and so much more.

Looking for Answers

As the weeks passed after my daughter's sexualized question, I began to wonder how other parents were handling digital parenting. So I did what any reasonable person would: I turned to social media for answers.

But instead of finding answers, I was bombarded with conflicting "expert" opinions.

"Respect your children's privacy. Don't look at their phones."

"Don't cave to peer pressure and give your child a phone."

To be honest, this advice made me feel judged. No matter what my husband and I did, someone would disagree with our parenting decisions. It was too much.

(Let's be honest: Is anyone on social media even qualified to give advice on how to parent kids with their own phones? I mean, we're the first generation of parents stumbling through this!)

I reminded myself that my daughter had been exposed to pornography in a conversation at school. No screens were present, and she didn't even have a phone at the time. She was at risk whether or not I allowed technology. I also began to notice that kids showed her things on their phones, or she'd look at their screens while she was hanging out with them at school or youth group.

The only way I could protect her was to change my parenting approach. I had to dig in and figure this out. So I doubled down on trying to find a solution that made sense. I read parenting books, talked to other parents, looked for answers in my Bible, and asked God to guide my search.

During that time, my husband and I made a huge decision.

Saying Yes to Technology

After much debate, discussion, and a lot of prayer, we finally decided to get our daughter a phone. It was time to face our fears head-on. We were ready to jump in and teach ourselves how to parent a phone, but it was a big decision we didn't take lightly.

Here are some of the questions we asked ourselves:

- As parents, are we ready to accept the additional responsibility of monitoring our child's phone?
- Is our child already telling us about inappropriate things she sees or hears?
- Does her school allow phones?
- Does she need a phone?

We figured that letting our daughter have her own device, with parental controls, would lessen the temptation to look at other kids' screens and reduce (but not eliminate) the likelihood of stumbling upon unfiltered content. We'd also have input on safety guidelines, restrictions, and apps. So getting her a phone seemed like a logical next step—and still does. We knew it wouldn't solve the problem, but we felt we were moving in the right direction.

All these years later, my husband and I are using the same logic as we teach our daughter to drive. We've discovered so many similarities. For example, by letting her drive a car we take care of, we have more input on things that will keep her safe, like regular maintenance and safety checks. We also reduce the likelihood that she'll ride in an unsafe vehicle with her friends. Does this mean she won't be in an accident or ride with friends in an unsafe car? No. But we know we're doing everything in our power to protect her and prepare her for life. That's our job as parents!

Starting slow is another similarity. The first day she got her driver's permit, she wanted to drive home. No way! She hadn't been behind the wheel of a car yet, and she would've had to go sixty-five miles per hour on one of our busiest highways. She wasn't ready for that, so we started in our neighborhood at twenty miles per hour. Let me tell you, we still almost ended up in a ditch! I'm not even kidding.

Whether it's a car or a phone, we've been teaching our daughter *one step at a time* to use each of these things responsibly. It's a process. Like handing her the car keys, we didn't just give our child a phone and say, "Have fun!"

Most of us learned to drive because our parents or another adult taught us. I have vivid memories of my grandpa teaching me to drive on the back roads of Indiana. But no one came alongside and taught us how to use a phone; we just dived in without any instruction. I think that's why we often miss the step-by-step process of teaching our kids. We just give them a phone, and that's it.

I've met so many good parents who are disappointed or angry with their children because of the choices they've made with their phones. But how can we expect them to use a phone responsibly without any real instruction?

My point is this: We have to teach our kids how to use a phone *step by step*. We're the first generation of parents who are figuring this out. We're writing the curriculum in real time.

Parenting a Phone

After getting our daughter a phone, the next step in the process was drawing up a contract all of us could sign that clearly explained our family guidelines and expectations. At first, our child wasn't allowed on social media. (That would've been like letting her drive sixty-five miles an hour the first time behind the wheel of our car!) No social media meant no apps to connect with online strangers. She could only text and FaceTime her friends and play games on a few basic apps.

After complying with our guidelines and reporting issues to us for several months, she earned the right to open one social media account at a time. It was a gradual process of building trust. (We're doing the same thing with driving. She gets to drive farther after she completes shorter trips safely.)

Even though my husband and I were learning to parent a phone as we walked through this process with our child, I realized it didn't solve the underlying problem. Yes, it reduced her exposure to other kids' content. And we were definitely preparing her for life. I felt good about that. But I discovered that restrictions didn't always work, and some things were much harder to monitor than others.

When someone mentioned a different solution, I perked up. *What if an app could mirror everything on my child's phone?* I wondered.

I researched and considered this solution for several weeks, but there were a couple of issues with it. First of all, kids text eight million emojis or abbreviations every day. So even if I had time to sort through them all, I'd have to look them up in the *Urban Dictionary* just to figure out what they stand for. Who has time for that?

There are also some operating systems and apps that prevent third-party monitoring. That may change over time with new laws, but right now, some access is limited.

But for the sake of argument, let's assume we could actually find a product on the market that does everything we need it to do for just $9.99 a month. For example, it gives us access to everything on our kids' phones.

Guess what? If our kids know we're monitoring their phones, *they'll just use a friend's phone instead.*

Loopholes.

I remember a school administrator telling me once, "There was a kid who had multiple phones in his locker, and he'd collect a fee for using them. His customers were other students who either wanted a second phone to hide their secret accounts or needed a phone because their parents had taken theirs away."

I envisioned this kid opening up his locker like a store and renting out his stash of phones. I was like "These kids are brilliant. That's the next Steve Jobs. He found a niche and created a business around it!" Ha!

We can lock down the phone and subscribe to every parental control on the market, but if our kids want to hide something from us, they'll find a way around our safety precautions. They're always one step ahead of us in the digital world, and we're always playing catch-up.

I'm not saying we shouldn't use all of the tools that are available to us. By all means, subscribe to the phone-monitoring apps. There are some excellent ones! Set restrictions and parental controls. Do random phone checks. Implement a phone contract with clear guidelines and consequences. Be in your kids' online world and follow them on social media.

These are all good and important things to do, but they don't actually solve the underlying problem.

"I Found the Solution!"

After finding weaknesses, flaws, and loopholes in different solutions I tried, I was frustrated and overwhelmed. I was learning how to parent technology, but I was no closer to finding an effective solution for keeping my kids safe online. Then I stumbled across the game changer.

One day I was sitting on the back porch reading my Bible. The verses were familiar; I had read them many times before. But this time was different. The words jumped right off the page:

> You must commit [yourself] wholeheartedly to these commands that I am giving you today. Repeat them again and again to your children. *TALK* about them when you are at home and *when you are on the road*, when you are going to bed and when you are getting up. (Deuteronomy 6:6-7, emphasis added)

The moment I read the words "talk ... when you are on the road," I knew I had found the solution. Oh my goodness, God knew!

I had already discovered that my kids *loved* asking me awkward questions *in the car* because they didn't have to look at me directly. I figured this approach could work to my advantage, too. For example, if my kids asked a question about sex while I was driving, I could be gripping the steering wheel and sweating profusely but calmly say, "Thank you for asking me this question. Let's talk about this." Ha!

The "on the road" point hit home, but that Bible passage actually lists *four* key times to talk with our kids:

1. When we're at home
2. When we're on the road
3. When we're getting up
4. When we're going to bed

I began to see how this practical approach to parenting could work in any situation. The solution was so simple, and it was right there in my Bible: *open communication. It was about having healthy, on-the-go conversations with my kids about the everyday issues and questions they struggle with.*

It wasn't about following a script or scheduling a family meeting where we'd talk to our kids about topics like sex and then check a box and never talk about the issue again. No. It was about open, honest conversations in real time!

That night I climbed into bed with my husband and squealed with excitement, "I figured it out! I found the solution! We have to talk with our kids about *everything*!"

After I explained what I meant, he said, "I don't know, Mandy. I don't feel comfortable talking to our young kids about sex. How do I do that? I don't want to overexpose them."

I felt deflated. He was right.

The next morning, I found myself thinking, *I'm already talking with my kids about what's going on in their world. I know who is crushing on whom and who's dropping f-bombs at recess. This solution is too simple. It's just common sense, right?*

A moment later, it seemed as if God was whispering in my ear, *Hey, Mandy, are you talking with your kids about that big scary picture I've shown you? Are you talking about pornography, online strangers, and sex trafficking? What about social media and sharing nudes?*

Immediately I got defensive. *How in the world am I supposed to do that?* I responded in my head. *My husband doesn't want to over-expose our kids, and neither do I.*

In my heart, I sensed His reply: *Let Me show you.*

That's when I committed to creating a new culture of open communication in our home. No topic would be off limits. I was going to give this a try and see if it really worked.

The next day, and every day since that moment, I've asked God to show me how to parent this technology problem. I've prayed specifically for teachable moments and intentional aware-ness so I won't miss what He wants me to see.

After seven years, I can tell you that when guidelines, filters, and restrictions didn't work, open communication did.

God had the solution all along. How like me to look every-where else first.

As parents, we can't always control the content on our kids' screens. But we can control the conversations we have about that content in our homes. Whether or not we allow our kids to have phones, the key to keeping them safe is open communication. This is our first line of defense.

Now that we've identified the problem and found a solution that works, let's talk about how we can implement it. I love this part because my understanding of open communication continues to deepen and evolve over time.

I can't wait to share some of the practical things God has been teaching me. So many times, He has stopped me in my tracks and shown me how to respond differently to my kids. I want you to see how Old Mandy transformed into New Mandy as I changed my parenting approach to match the shift that's taken place in our digital world.

I know this "talk to your kids" solution sounds so simple. But as you'll soon discover, open communication isn't just about talking. It's about building a whole new culture of conversation so our children will feel safe telling us what they're seeing and hearing online.

3

TEN PRACTICAL IDEAS FOR IMPLEMENTING THE SOLUTION

I'm convinced that open communication is the solution for keeping our kids safe in today's digital world. Filters and restrictions fail, but real-time conversations work. I've seen open communication protect my kids over and over again. Like when my son jumps into the car after school and says, "I heard this today. What does it mean?"

No filter will catch the conversations kids have at the school lunch table or on the bus about what they saw on their screens the night before. But having a healthy dialogue does.

I have to be honest with you: Implementing this solution involves some hard work. But I promise it's worth the effort!

There isn't a cookie-cutter approach to open communication or a universal script to follow. Your child's questions will be different from my child's questions. And as parents, we may differ on how to handle some topics. That's okay! I respect your right to make decisions for your own family. Your family, your choice. The examples I share in this chapter are only to give you an idea of what open communication looks like in our family.

Even if we have different views about how to parent difficult issues, let's not miss the solution: *creating a healthy dialogue with our kids.*

Creating a New Culture

As I've walked this path with my own kids, I've discovered that open communication is about more than just having a few conversations here and there. We actually need to create a *culture* of honest conversation. But how do we do that?

In this chapter, I'll share ten practical ideas for creating this new culture. I'll also share some of the valuable lessons God has taught me through this process. I want to be transparent with you about what I'm learning. Notice I said *learning.* I'm not an expert. (I cringe when people call me that!) I'm just a mom in the trenches with you, fighting through the challenges and learning to navigate this problem in real time.

Remember what I shared in the previous chapter about the process my husband and I followed when we got our daughter a phone? Little by little, we taught ourselves how to navigate the digital world and parent a phone. We were figuring this thing out one step at a time.

We drew up a phone contract with family guidelines and consequences, set restrictions, and monitored our child's phone use. But more importantly, we started having real-time conversations with our daughter. We were involved in her online world, walking hand in hand as we learned together. Throughout the process, we were building trust. And I was learning an important lesson: keeping my child safe online is more about relationship than rules.

When our daughter earned her first social media platform (by showing us inappropriate content she'd found on another app), it felt amazing! I went to bed thinking *We rocked that! This works!* I could feel the tide turning. We didn't parent it perfectly, but we were making progress.

Everything was going well. Then I encountered my first big test.

Old Mandy versus New Mandy

One evening as I was making tacos for dinner, my then thirteen-year-old turned the corner into the kitchen, phone in her hand with eyes wide open. I was in the middle of chopping up tomatoes while the meat sautéed. I remember this detail because I burned the tacos that night, and we ended up having shells with tomatoes and cheese. I am not kidding!

When I saw the expression on her face, I knew something big was about to happen.

I breathed a silent prayer: *Okay, Lord, I've been praying every day for intentional conversations with my daughter. Help me. Don't let me lose my mind when I see what she's about to show me.*

My daughter walked over and said, "I was scrolling through my Instagram feed looking at some pictures of a wedding my friends went to. The pictures of the bride and the bridesmaids' dresses were gorgeous. In their post, they included a wedding hashtag [#wedding], so I clicked to see more dresses, and this popped up."

She shoved her screen in front of my face, and this is what I saw: Naked. Women. On beds. In weird positions.

I paused.

Old Mandy would've grabbed the phone, thrown it in the trash, and said, "I tried to be cool Insta-mom. But this is the Devil's playground. NO! NO! NO! We're done!"

Much to my surprise, I did none of that. Who was this new person?

New Mandy gently took the phone and placed it facedown on the kitchen counter. Then I looked my baby girl in the eyes and calmly said, "I'm so proud of you. You did nothing wrong. You were trying to look at dresses, and Satan wanted you to see bad things. But you told me. You did everything right. Because you're telling me about what you're seeing online, you can pick out a new app today. Tell me what you want; then I'll research it and see if it's age appropriate."

Old Mandy had inadvertently created an environment where my kids wanted to hide the bad things they saw online because they knew I'd delete the app or throw away the phone. I didn't even know I was shutting down communication. New Mandy is learning to encourage my kids to tell me what they're seeing and hearing online. They even get rewarded when they do!

After this conversation, I took my daughter's phone into another room and reported the pornography to Instagram so it could be taken down. You guys, I found even more pictures than the ones my child had been exposed to, and I was struggling to process it all. In the days that followed, I had honest conversations with my girl about it. I'd crawl into bed with her at night (remember Deuteronomy 6:7?) and say, "I'm struggling to get those images out of my head."

I can't even tell you how much conversation that created. It opened up a whole new dialogue about why images like that are bad for us, and how they cause us to look at people as objects instead of seeing their hearts. These honest conversations were way more likely to prevent my kid from watching pornography than just yelling "No!" and throwing away the phone. I saw firsthand that relationship is so much more effective than rules.

Old Mandy would have missed the opportunity to have any of these conversations.

Ten Practical Ideas for Creating a Culture of Conversation

There's so much I could share with you about creating a culture of conversation in our families, but the following ten ideas have helped me the most. This is where we put open communication into practice.

1. Avoid Crazy-Parent Mode

When we overreact, we shut down conversation. When we throw phones in the trash because our kids saw porn, it creates a barrier. When we lecture for twenty minutes, we unintentionally build walls, and our kids tune us out. If we rant and rave, they're less likely to confide in us. But by responding calmly, we can create a healthy dialogue.

If you're thinking, *Great. I was just in crazy-parent mode five minutes ago*, do not beat yourself up. I still struggle with this! Sometimes my son will see the look on my face and say, "You're trying not to go into crazy-mom mode, aren't you?"

If you've messed up recently, it's a perfect opportunity to work on creating a culture of open communication in your family. Start off by offering an apology. (If I'm being honest, I kinda hope you *have* gone into crazy-parent mode, because apologies are so good for setting a new tone with kids.)

Circle back by saying, "Remember when I went crazy after you showed me ____? I'm so sorry. I didn't handle that well. I was mad about what you saw, but I wasn't mad at you. In fact, I'm really proud that you told me. That's what I always want you to do." An apology goes a long way with our kids.

Then start some healthy conversations about why you were so upset. Help your kids understand *why* the content is bad for them. But remember: this is not a lecture; it's a dialogue.

One of my favorite parenting verses is "Be quick to listen, slow to speak, and slow to get angry" (James 1:19). New Mandy is learning to put that verse into practice by removing my feelings from the equation and asking God to guide my response, especially when I'm upset.

We need to pause and pray *before* we act.

If we can put this into practice when our kids are young, they'll be more likely to confide the life-altering issues they're dealing with when they're older. For example, if you stay calm and avoid going into crazy-parent mode when they tell you about someone using the f-word at recess, it will be standard operating procedure for them to tell you when their friends are cutting, sharing nudes, and watching pornography. Once you've proven that you can control your emotions with the little things, your kids will feel safe telling you about the bigger issues.

Recently I received feedback from an out-of-state event host I met last year when I spoke at a community event he arranged. Here's what he shared:

A dad finds porn on his sixth grader's devices. Doesn't lose his mind. Starts an incredible dialogue with his kid about his own struggles and morality, and kid opens up.

43

Relationship strengthened rather than kid being pushed away. I love hearing these stories. nextTalk for the win!

Nothing shuts down communication faster than flying into crazy-parent mode. But staying calm can lead to many great discussions with our children and help to keep them safer in this digital world.

Remember when we talked about YouTube and how kids imitate the behaviors they watch on their screens, like eating Tide Pods? Instead of going into crazy-parent mode when our kids imitate a questionable or dangerous behavior, we can take advantage of this teachable moment and have a meaningful conversation with them.

It's important to connect what we're learning to what we're trying to teach our kids about thinking before they imitate a behavior. For example, you could say something like this: "You know how I'm learning not to launch into crazy-parent mode? I have to pause first and think through how I'm going to respond. YouTube is the same way. When you watch something on a screen, pause first and think through how you're going to respond. Before you imitate a behavior, make sure it isn't dangerous or harmful."

The lessons we're learning as parents often relate to thought processes we need to teach our kids!

2. Create a Safe Place

To build a culture of conversation in your home, you need to prove that you're worthy of your kids' trust. They need a safe place to process all they're being exposed to. I want it to be you.

For example, if your son is crushing on someone, do NOT post about it on social media. If your daughter just started shaving her legs, don't announce it to your friend group. My cohost on our next-Talk podcast says, "Don't broadcast their business." I love that!

I know not to broadcast my husband's business, because I respect his privacy. But do I give my kids that same level of respect?

You can earn your kids' trust by respecting them and keeping their confidences. They are little souls you've been entrusted with, and they need to know they can talk about their feelings and ask awkward questions without worrying that you'll text your friend group or post their confidences for the world to see.

Be the place where they can share their struggles over things like feeling rejected on social media, longing for deeper friendships, or questioning their sexuality. If you are their safe place, maybe they'll be less likely to turn to things like cutting to numb their pain and will talk to you instead. Then you can help them process their feelings in a healthy way.

Tell your child, "I'm your safe space. Your secrets and questions are safe with me. And no matter what you share with me, I promise to always love you. I won't yell or get mad. I just want to help you process whatever you're going through."

If you want to truly be their safe place, make sure your actions match your words.

When my daughter hit middle school, I made a deal with her that I'd ask permission if I wanted to post something about her on social media—even bragging posts. I do that with both of my kids now. I don't share *anything* without their permission. That includes stories I share in my books, on podcasts, at events, or in videos. They deleted some good stories from this book (trust me, you're missing out on some crazy ones), but building a safe place for them is more important to me. Remember that highly sexualized question my daughter asked that started this whole thing? I didn't share the exact question with you because she asked me not to, and I wanted her to know she can trust me.

Building trust is so important. If you don't, your kids won't talk to you. One way we protect confidences in our family is by designating the special things we share as "just-us stories." These might be surprise gifts, sweet handwritten notes, or embarrassing but hilarious moments. For example, when something happens, I'll be like "Can I post that, or is it a just-us story?" Sometimes my kids beat me to it. As they're laughing at themselves, they'll say, "This is definitely a just-us story."

Sharing things online without your kids' permission can damage the trust and open communication you've worked so hard to build. Everything they share with you should be kept in strictest confidence. I mean *everything*! Prove to them you can be trusted.

I have to warn you: If you've been effective at creating open communication, you'll hear some really tough stuff. You're going to know which kids are having sex or being bullied, who is using drugs, and who is self-harming or talking about suicide. What you hear will shock and even scare you. Just remember that you're trying to build trust and be a safe place for your kids.

What if your child tells you about a dangerous or life-threatening situation another child is involved in? Should you break the confidence and let someone else know? I have to be real with you: this the hardest part of creating open communication.

Each situation is different, so we can't make one rule that applies to every scenario. But we can set some basic guidelines. For example, if a child's life is at risk, whether from suicide, cyberbullies, or online strangers, we have a duty to speak up.

How I handle these kinds of situations has shifted, though. For example, Old Mandy would have swooped in to save the day if my child told me that someone was being bullied at school. I would have emailed the entire school administration and maybe even posted something on Facebook.

New Mandy is aware that I have to protect my kids. "Snitches get stitches" is a real threat. We don't want our kids to get bullied for reporting. But we also need to teach them to speak up. Here's where healthy conversation comes in. I might say something like "Because we know this information, it's important we speak up. How would we feel if something bad happened to this child? So here are some options: We can text this anonymous number at your school, I can email a school administrator and ask that your name be kept out of it, or you can talk to a teacher directly. How would you like to handle it?"

New Mandy doesn't swoop in. I bring my kids into the decision-making process and empower them to step up and do the right thing because it's the right thing. Then I go back to them and say, "Your courage got this child help. I'm so proud of you." Sometimes I can even say, "Honey, you probably saved this child's life."

New Mandy is learning to use these moments to teach valuable life lessons.

3. Adopt a No-Secrets Family Policy

Establishing a no-secrets family policy is essential for protecting our kids from a myriad of things, but in this section, I want to specifically focus on how it can protect them from sex trafficking, grooming, and sexual abuse.

Teach your children as early as possible that your family policy is to never keep secrets from each other. I say to my kids, "We have no secrets in our family!"

As we discussed earlier, online sex traffickers often use a profile picture of a kid around the same age as your child so they can build a secret online relationship. To get your child to share secrets, they may say things like "My mom just gets on my nerves. She doesn't understand!" The more secrets your child shares, the more likely it will progress to sharing nudes. Then the blackmail starts, and your child may be trafficked from his or her own bedroom or coerced into meeting the pimp in person.

A no-secrets policy can prevent your child from being trafficked.

Although sexual abuse can happen with complete strangers, research shows that most kids are abused by someone they know.

In fact, according to the National Institute of Justice, "nearly three in four adolescents (74 percent) |report| that |an| assault was committed by someone they knew well."[8]

When my kids were little, I'd say things like "Don't let *anyone* touch your private parts." That's good, but children tend to think of a stranger or even a big green scary monster trying to touch their private parts. The research shows that it's likely to be a favorite teacher, a coach, a pastor, or even a family member who tries to touch them inappropriately. This betrayal catches a child completely off guard.

Adults (and even other children) who want to groom kids for sexual abuse will form connections with them and try to establish trust. For example, a groomer might drop an f-bomb in a conversation and say, "Don't tell your parents."

If your child keeps the secret, the next step is getting him or her to engage in some kind of mildly bad behavior, like drinking alcohol. The groomer might say, "I have alcohol in my cooler. Have you ever tried it? I'll give you one little sip, but you can't tell your parents! I'd get in so much trouble." If your child keeps that secret, too, it's a green light for the groomer to move to the next step: sharing nudes with your child. (Remember the "dick pics" from chapter 1?)

Groomers will often share and/or ask for nudes to test a child before things get physical in a face-to-face encounter. If your child keeps these secrets, a groomer knows he can probably get away with more abuse.

Do you see how a scenario like this could be prevented with a no-secrets family policy? It can literally save your child from being physically or sexually abused. Make sure to discuss this policy continually with your kids so it becomes engrained in their minds and hearts.

I do have one disclaimer: When you implement a no-secrets policy, you're going to hear all kinds of crazy things from your kids. So you have to be careful not to be dismissive or overreact.

One time my child said, "The teacher told us to put our heads on the desk and sleep for fifteen minutes, but not to tell our parents."

I was thinking, *I would've let them sleep the entire class period!* But I didn't want to dismiss what my child was reporting. So instead, I praised my child for telling me and replied with a stoplight analogy that a friend shared with me: "I don't think your teacher is a bad person, but let's move her from a green light to a yellow light. If she asks you to keep any other secrets from me, will you tell me?"

You may also need to explain your policy to other people, including well-meaning family members.

That happened when we invited my husband's parents and my mom to join our family for a trip to an amusement park. Before heading to the water park, my husband and I left the kids with the grandparents to get our bathing suits and towels in the car. As we walked away, we said, "No more sweets because we're getting ready to swim."

When we returned, my son was acting a little strange. He finally pulled me aside and said, "Grandma got us a funnel cake and told us not to tell you."

Here I was, trying to teach my kids not to keep secrets from us, and Grandma told them not to tell us about a stupid funnel cake?

I was furious, but responding to my mom in crazy-*daughter* mode wasn't going to help the situation, so I didn't react in the moment.

The next day, after having a calm conversation with my husband, I called my mom and explained the situation. I said, "I don't think I've done a good job explaining to you about this new path we're on. Kids are being exposed to pornography in elementary school, and they're being groomed by sex traffickers online. I'm trying to get our kids to always be honest with us and tell us everything. I know you didn't mean anything by it, but we don't have any secrets in our home. I want you to spoil your grandkids and don't ever want to take that away from you. But in the future, would you please not tell our kids to keep secrets from us?"

My mom broke down in tears. She just didn't know. She offered to talk to the kids and let them know that telling them to keep a secret from me was wrong.

I share this because it's a community issue. We must stop using cute little sayings like "What happens at Grandma's stays at Grandma's." It's confusing to kids, and we're not being consistent if we're trying to get them to tell us everything. I've even been at church youth events where I've heard leaders say, "Don't tell your parents you ate that much sugar."

Cringe! I know it's just sugar, but we all need to be on the same page to protect our kids.

When I share this example at events, someone usually asks, "What if my daughter asks me not to tell her dad about something she's shared with me?"

The way we handle this in our home seems to work well. If my daughter is talking to me in confidence and says, "Please don't tell Dad," I reply, "Mom and Dad don't have secrets. The Bible says that a husband and wife are one. So I'm going to be honest with Dad, but I'm going to tell him you're not comfortable talking about this with him." Then my husband always respects that boundary.

Now that my son is getting older, sometimes he talks to my husband more than he talks to me. After a conversation, my husband will tell me what's going on, but I respect my son's boundaries. Old Mandy would've been like "Soooo, I've heard you're crushing on _____." New Mandy waits until my son brings it up with me.

No secrets in your family will protect your kids from so many things. And it can prevent smaller problems from becoming major crises.

A counselor I work with closely told me, "I love what you're doing. On a scale of 0 to 10, with 10 being the place where crisis happens, you and nextTalk are creating conversations at 1, 2, and 3. Those conversations will often prevent a 10 from ever happening."

I love that illustration!

My passion is to prevent kids from being exposed to harmful influences in the first place, which is why I hope to reach more families with younger kids. This is about prevention. The earlier we create an atmosphere of open communication in our homes, the more likely we'll be to avoid a crisis.

4. Answer Your Kids' Questions

When I was growing up and had a question about sex, I'd look in the encyclopedia (I'm so old!), or I'd ask my friends and often get misinformation. If our kids have a question about sex, where do they turn?

Google.

For example, if they want to know what a *blow job* is, they look it up online. (I'm sorry if this makes you blush, but if we can't use these words with each other, we won't be able to answer our kids' questions.)

So what will they see when the search results pop up on the screen? Videos of male-female and male-male oral sex.

That may be shocking to you, but this is one of the ways pornography has changed. (Remember that discussion in chapter 1?)

Now imagine that you're driving your ten-year-old to soccer practice, and he yells from the back of the car, "What does *blow job* mean?"

If my child had asked a question like that when I was Old Mandy, I would've died. Cringed. Screamed. Or driven off the road and wrecked the car.

New Mandy stays calm and thinks, *I just protected my kid from pornography and all the confusion it brings. God knew. Open communication works!*

We need to shift our thinking.

Instead of being mortified that your kids are asking questions like these, be thankful you're their safe place.

Be your child's Google. Continually tell your kids, "Not everything you hear on the playground or read online is true. When you're curious about something or hear a new word you don't understand, ask me. Never search online."

If your child asks a question you don't know the answer to, or if you aren't sure how to answer the question in age-appropriate terms, buy some time to find the answer or figure out how much to share. Here are a few ways you can do that:

- It's perfectly okay to say, "Can I have a day to pray about this? I want to give you the right information." My personal rule is to get back to my kids in twenty-four hours. This shows them that their questions matter.
- You could also say, "We need to cover a few other things before we talk about this topic." For example, before defining oral and anal sex, set a foundation for that conversation by telling your child how babies are formed (i.e., egg and sperm). Kids today are often exposed to more advanced sexual topics at much younger ages, which means we need to start the first sex talk earlier. These talks will become ongoing discussions that will get more detailed as your kids get older.
- If your child's question includes a slang word, and you don't know what it means, tell your child that you need to

do some research first. Then Google the word later (but not in front of your child). Use technology to your advantage. I probably consult the *Urban Dictionary* more than my kids do!

- Lighten things up and have fun. Our family sings a little song we made up: "Scarred for life. Scarred for life. Everybody, everybody's scarred for life." We do a little dance, too. So if one of my kids asks me something really out there, I might say, "I don't want to scar you for life, so you're gonna have to give me a minute." Make it fun! Kids love this.

Above all, don't ignore your kids' questions or sweep them under the rug. If you're not ready to give an answer right away, explain why. Make a point of acknowledging that your kids' curiosity is natural, and you're their go-to source for information.

Every question your child asks is an opportunity to build more open communication in your home. Take advantage of it!

5. Set Family Screen Guidelines

Setting family guidelines for screens is important because children need to know what's expected of them. It seems simple, but sometimes we miss this step because no one taught us how to use a phone or gave us guidelines.

Think about your preschooler barging into the bathroom with a diaper on, sippy cup in one hand and your phone (or a tablet) in the other. He comes in shouting, "Mommy! Mommy!" because you get no privacy ever with a toddler, right? And the drool. It's everywhere! I can't.

(I would take five hundred teens over one toddler. Bless you, parents of little ones!)

As parents, we often miss this teachable moment with our preschoolers. But now that we're no longer afraid of the new problem, we can use moments like these to plant seeds because we know that nude photos will be an issue in the future, right?

So instead of overreacting to the bathroom incident or ignoring it altogether, you can use it as a teachable moment and calmly say to your child, "Did you know that phone takes pictures? Oh no! What if you accidentally took a picture of mommy without clothes on? That would be awful! We never take pictures of people without clothes on. So from now on, we're not bringing screens into the bathroom."

You just planted a seed with your preschooler for future conversations about nudes without exposing him to anything inappropriate for his age. You're being proactive, not reactive. You're not only learning to create screen guidelines to keep him safe, but you're also having preventive conversations and laying the groundwork for more detailed discussions as your child gets older.

Old Mandy missed teachable moments like these. New Mandy is looking for them.

As you create these new guidelines, you'll also have to practice what you preach. For example, one time my son was taking a bubble bath, and he looked so adorable covered in bubbles that I snapped a photo of him. I was going to text it to my husband, but then my son reminded me of our no-screens bathroom rule.

I replied, "You're absolutely right. I broke the rule, and that was a big mistake on my part. I'm sorry!"

Other family guidelines we've set for our kids are no screens in bedrooms or at meals, no downloading of new apps without a parent's approval, no password changes without telling us, and no security- or privacy-setting changes unless they ask. (You can find more guidelines in our sample phone contract by texting CELLPHONE to 44222. For information on phones, contracts, and social media, read these chapters in *TALK* or listen to the nextTalk podcasts.)

Once you have your own family screen guidelines in place, make sure to explain them clearly to your kids. Keep in mind that your guidelines will change over time, especially as your kids get older and earn more freedom. This isn't a one and done. If you gradually give your children more freedom in the digital world, they'll begin to develop a healthy balance with screens and will hopefully be able to self-regulate when they leave home.

One of my former pastors used a kite string to illustrate building trust. As our children earn our trust by following the guidelines we set, we can let out more string so they can fly higher. If they mess up or stumble, we reel them in to correct and teach them. When they demonstrate growth, we give them more string (freedom) again. I love that analogy.

When our kids were smaller, our guideline was absolutely no screens in bedrooms—ever. Now we give our sixteen-year-old daughter more freedom because she's older and we know we can trust her. Virtual learning during the COVID pandemic has forced us to set up workstations throughout our home, so now she has a laptop in her bedroom. (She also has a pet bunny in her bedroom with its own Instagram account, so pictures and videos are needed!)

Younger kids shouldn't be allowed the same amount of freedom we give older teens. They need to earn that freedom as they show they can handle more independence. At thirteen, my son doesn't have nearly the phone independence my sixteen-year-old has. And he doesn't have a laptop in his bedroom for virtual learning. When he complains, I say, "You'll have to earn the freedom too."

Guidelines are still important for older children, but as they prepare to launch into life, they should be learning to regulate their own screen use without needing you to constantly remind them of the rules.

One time, my daughter decided entirely on her own to take a break from Instagram. I was so proud! That's a win. Tell your kids how proud you are of them when you see them creating their own healthy balance with screens. As my daughter continued her Instagram break, I asked her if she noticed any changes. She said, "I'm less distracted while doing homework, and I feel less pressure." She's teaching herself, so I don't need to remind her of our guidelines as often.

When my kids first got phones, random phone checks happened daily or weekly. Now that our daughter is older, they're not as often. If I started seeing mood swings or other issues, I'd increase the number of phone checks. But she's just a few years from moving out of the house, so I want to prepare her to navigate this on her own.

At some point, your kids will "age out" of screen guidelines, as one of our nextTalk team members calls it. As a parent, you have to think ahead. You don't want your teen or young adult texting you from her first job and asking, "Can I download this new app?" This is a guideline your kids should age out of as they get older.

When your children move out of the house, will they be able to manage their own screen time?

A parent at one of our events asked me, "What phone-monitoring software do you recommend to see texts and bad comments on social media?" I asked how old her kid was, and she said, "Nineteen."

Guys, our kids need independence at nineteen! If we teach them how to self-regulate and have a healthy balance now, they'll experience success as they launch out on their own. Will they call us for advice when they're off balance? Absolutely! And we'll walk them through it. But we must push them toward independence, letting the string out gradually so they can learn to fly on their own.

One guideline in our family that doesn't age out is sleeping with screens. We still don't allow our sixteen-year-old to have her phone with her at bedtime.

It's especially important to explain the *why* behind this guideline. When my kids ask why it doesn't change as they get older, I say something like "I want this to become a healthy habit because screen addiction is real. Doctors say that screens at bedtime are bad for our brains, and they recommend turning them off before bed so we're able to rest. We need sleep for good health. I'm hoping that when you move out, you'll make it a point to not sleep with your phones." My reasoning comes from the American Academy of Pediatrics: "All screens [should] be turned off 30 minutes before bedtime and that TV, computers and other screens not be allowed in children's bedrooms."[9]

Deciding how and when to change your family screen guidelines depends on a number of factors, including whether your children are following the guidelines already in place and whether they've earned your trust by reporting things to you. You know your kids better than anyone else. If you notice red flags, reel in the kite string and place more restrictions on screen time.

6. Explain What to Report

This sounds like common sense, but in an online world where everything is snapped, posted, and shared, kids often don't know what content is appropriate or inappropriate. That's why you need to be clear about your expectations.

Here are some of the reporting guidelines we follow in our home:

- *Share with us anything you see online about dating, kissing, and marriage.* I've had a lot of great conversations with my kids when I've asked them to report this kind of content to me. That doesn't mean it's necessarily bad, though we have caught some inappropriate content. It could be two teddy bears getting married on a 4-plus app, your child's favorite YouTuber talking about his girlfriend, or an ad with two men in bed together. (Remember the bunny app? This guideline is why my son told me about that pop-up!)

- *Ask about any words you don't know or understand.* This guideline is important to implement when your kids are little and then apply to their online world when they're older. Say to them, "When you hear a new word or phrase, ask me about it. Never search online." With my kids, I also add, "Or you'll be scarred for life," and then we bust out dancing to our little rap. Make this fun!

- *Report any violence, bullying, threatening, or mean language.* This guideline is also important because it sends a red-flag alert to your child's brain to report harmful or dangerous online content or situations to you. Without a guideline in place, your child might not report these kinds of things. If your child tells you, "I was playing Xbox with my friends the other day, and one of them called me stupid," remain calm and avoid texting the other parent. Instead, ask, "How did that make you feel?"

One time I thought my son was being bullied on Fortnite because another child cussed him out. When

I pushed into more-detailed discussions, I discovered that my son had kicked this other boy out of a party on Fortnite, and that kid felt rejected. Should he have cussed out my son? No. But by having a healthy dialogue with my son about it, I was able to show him that the way he treated this child escalated the situation.

- *Report any cusswords.* Again, this is something to initiate when your kids are young and then apply to their online world as they get older. If your child repeats a cussword he or she heard but clearly doesn't understand, remain calm and talk about why you don't use words like that. You could even say, "Different families have different guidelines. In our family, that's a word we don't use because we couldn't use it on a job interview. So why start a bad habit?"

- *Report any person who asks you for personal information.* This is one of the most important conversations to have with your kids. Emphasize that your child should ALWAYS tell you if *anyone* (whether face-to-face or online) asks for personal details like your home address or where your child goes to school or church. This could literally save your child from sex traffickers, groomers, pedophiles, or anyone else with illicit or evil motives.

- *Report anyone in a bathing suit or less.* My husband and I set this guideline for bathing-suit pictures when our kids were little. That doesn't mean we think all bathing-suit pictures are bad, but that was our threshold.

When my son was younger, he Googled a football score while he was sitting at our kitchen island. Suddenly he yelled, "There's a girl on a motorcycle, and she has a little string in her butt. That's all she's wearing." This guideline is the reason he told me!

Without shaming the girl, I simply said to him, "I'm so proud of you for telling me." Then we talked about the importance of protecting our hearts and minds and not looking at girls as objects. (I go into more detail about this in the pornography chapter in *TALK*.)

As our kids have gotten older, our guidelines have changed. They've aged out. Now that we've talked about the difference between an innocent bathing-suit picture and a sexual pose in a teeny-weeny string bikini, our kids only report the highly sexualized pictures to us.

7. Teach Your Kids to Protect Their Hearts and Minds

We aren't with our children 24/7, so we need to teach them the importance of not allowing harmful thoughts and images into their hearts and minds. They have to self-manage what they allow in.

Ever since our daughter's exposure to porn in the fourth grade, my husband and I have been teaching our kids to guard their hearts and minds. They know they're responsible for what they look at, listen to, think about, download, search for, comment on, and participate in. They also know they're ultimately responsible to God.

If another kid tells my son about the hot women he saw on "Ph" (Pornhub) the night before, I don't want my child to think, *My parents will kill me if I Google that.* Instead, I pray he'll think, *Is this good for my heart and mind?*

When my son was in elementary school, some kids at the lunch table started talking about oral sex while another child was eating a Popsicle. They didn't use the words *oral sex*, but they were describing it in detail. Yes, I'm serious!

When I picked my son up from school, he told me about it before we were even out of the school parking lot. Then he said, "I need to know what they were talking about. What is this?"

We had previously set the foundation for a conversation about this topic by talking about how babies are made, so I was ready to explain it. But as I started to answer his question, he raised his hand, put it in front of my face, and said, "STOP! I want to protect my heart and mind."

Y'all, my heart melted! My son had learned to advocate for himself and not allow pictures or details to enter his mind that he wasn't ready for yet. I was so proud of him.

Old Mandy just wanted to bubble-wrap my kids and shield them from the world. New Mandy is teaching them to protect their *own* hearts and minds as they prepare for life in this broken world.

This concept comes straight from Scripture:

Guard your heart above all else,
for it determines the course of your life. (Proverbs 4:23)

From the heart come evil thoughts, murder, adultery, all sexual immorality, theft, lying, and slander. (Matthew 15:19)

I will set no worthless thing before my eyes. (Psalm 101:3, NASB)

I love that!

These are just a few relevant Bible verses you can share with your child. Another excellent resource for kids six years of age and up is *Good Pictures, Bad Pictures: Porn Proofing Today's Young Kids* by Kristen Jenson. I found this resource incredibly helpful when I was teaching my kids to protect their hearts and minds from pornography, but it's useful for many other topics, too. Kristen has also written *Good Pictures, Bad Pictures Jr.* for children under six.

8. Teach Your Kids to Develop a Moral Compass and Default to Love

Just as teachers on the first day of school define the ground rules for student behavior, we need to teach our children the difference between right and wrong. Without a moral compass, kids think that everything goes. When there are no boundaries, lines are blurred and confusion sets in.

As parents, we get to choose which morals or beliefs to teach our children. Your family, your choice.

I'm talking about life decisions here. For example, when is it okay to have sex, and with whom? You may have to dig deep to figure out what you believe, but this is important. Don't avoid these topics, I beg you. Our kids are drowning, and there is so much confusion. If you don't address issues like these, someone else will. By talking about them, you have the chance to be a strong influencer and educator in your child's life.

Our family defines right and wrong based on our faith. It helps us know which lines not to cross. You may have different views about what's morally acceptable or how to handle conversations about boundaries. That's okay. We can respectfully disagree and still be kind to one another.

Once you dive into these difficult conversations with your kids, you may notice them becoming judgmental if another child has a different belief or boundary. When you see that judgmental tone seeping in, remind your kids that we are to treat others the way we want to be treated.

No matter how you define your moral compass, here's where I think we can find common ground: Let's teach our kids to default to love. This is an important life skill we should model in this extremely divisive and hateful world.

When I speak in public schools or at secular community events, this is where I stop. However, at church events or private schools where I'm speaking to a predominantly Christian audience, I have a lot more to say.

As a follower of Jesus, I base my moral compass on the truth found in the Bible, even when that truth is unpopular. Instead of running from a topic that's uncomfortable, we need to press into it. (*Note:* If the following discussion doesn't reflect your beliefs, feel free to skip to the next point.)

I'm seriously concerned about the silence surrounding sex, sexuality, and transgender in our Christian community. And when we do tackle these topics, do we love like Jesus?

I know these are controversial issues, but if we can't talk about them with each other, we won't talk about them with our kids. I firmly believe that the reason people are walking away from the faith is, in part, because Christians are afraid to have real conversations about real issues, and when we do, our tone doesn't reflect the truth in Scripture.

Let's revisit the topic of sexuality for a moment. (For a more detailed discussion about sex, sexuality, and transgender, check out those chapters in *TALK*.)

Remember in chapter 1 when my eleven-year-old asked, "What does *bisexual* mean?"

I'm ashamed to admit this, but Old Mandy probably would've responded with something like "Those kids are just confused. Don't be mean, but stay away from that crowd."

To my embarrassment, I can see now that some of Old Mandy's responses weren't right or biblical, including this one. New Mandy defaulted to love and encouraged my child to be kind to everyone and speak up if anyone was being disrespectful or making fun of a child who identified as bisexual. Later on, we circled back for a longer conversation, and I explained the definition of *bisexual*. As you can imagine, that elicited a lot of discussion with my curious sixth grader.

I'm learning that when I get questions like "Is this okay?" it's often better to start the conversation by saying, "I don't get to tell people how to live. Who am I? I get things wrong all the time. But there is One who has the authority to tell us how to live. Why don't we look this up in the Bible and see what God says about it?"

Because the Bible defines our boundaries, we don't have to figure out what is right and wrong. The Bible gives us that clarity. Sometimes we'll read Scripture together, or now that our kids are older, I might give them verses to look up so they can discover the answer on their own.

I could point to several Old and New Testament verses that relate to sexuality (many of them are included in *TALK*), but I love the simplicity of this passage:

> Because there is so much sexual immorality, each man should have his own wife, and each woman should have her own husband. The husband should fulfill his wife's sexual needs, and the wife should fulfill her husband's needs. (1 Corinthians 7:2–3)

After my kids read the verses I've given them, I'll ask, *What does God say about this?*

I want them to see for themselves what God says. This teaches them to dig into Scripture for answers to real issues and helps them develop real faith. It's different from me just barking out opinions or answers. I don't make the rules; God does. He's our moral compass.

Once my kids know what God has to say about an issue, the next question they need to ask is, *Am I going to submit to His truth or not?*

As Jackie Hill Perry, the author of *Gay Girl, Good God*, said on Twitter, "You'll surrender anything when you believe God is everything." (That's a good book, by the way!)

What if our kids ask, "Why can't two people who love each other just love each other?"

Here's how I've learned to respond: "That's a really good question. Do you remember when we talked about the hashtag 'Love is love' that's trending on social media? That sounds like a great hashtag, but does it apply in every situation? What if a married man wants to date a woman who isn't his wife? There needs to be a moral compass so the lines don't get blurred. Do you see that? Boundaries protect us."

I've also said, "Do you remember when you asked for Snapchat in third grade, and I said no? It wasn't because I hated you and wanted to make your life miserable. It's because I wanted to protect you. I wanted to keep you safe. That's how God is with us. He gives us restrictions because He wants to protect us."

In Isaiah 55:8, God says, "My thoughts are nothing like your thoughts.... And my ways are far beyond anything you could imagine." We may not always understand God's restrictions, but we can trust that He has our best interests at heart.

I've learned that God will equip us with the words to say if we're fully submitted to Him. By studying the Word and knowing what we believe, we can guide our children and help them develop a moral compass based on God's truth.

Satan wants us to stay silent. Silence creates confusion and becomes a stumbling block that keeps our kids from developing deep-rooted, authentic faith.

As I pointed out earlier, when we teach our children to distinguish right from wrong, there's a danger they'll become judgmental. This is a problem we must address.

No matter the circumstances, default to love and always "treat people the same way you want them to treat you" (Matthew 7:12, NASB). (Did you know this Golden Rule actually originated with Jesus?)

We cannot cling to the biblical truth that "marriage is between a man and a woman" and yet abandon the truth of loving our neighbors. No! It's both. If our kids see us preaching the Golden Rule in public and then slandering LGBTQ+ people behind closed doors, it teaches them to be hypocritical. Our kids have LGBTQ+ people in their lives, and it is our responsibility to teach them not only what the Bible says about marriage but also to love like Jesus. The last thing we want to do is raise little bully Pharisees. (Those were the religious, holier-than-thou leaders back in Jesus's day.)

In John 8, we see how judgmental the Pharisees actually were. They had just caught a woman in the act of adultery and dragged her in front of a group of people Jesus was teaching.

This woman was guilty of sexual sin. It's important to note that sexual sin is sexual sin whether it's a male and female outside of marriage, two males, two females, a threesome, or any other combination that doesn't reflect God's blueprint. You get the point. God's Word tells us that "sexual immorality is a *sin* against your own body" (1 Corinthians 6:18, emphasis added).

After the Pharisees brought the woman to Jesus, they announced, "This woman was caught in the act of adultery. The law of Moses says to stone her. What do you say?" (John 8:4–5).

Jesus was quiet for a moment.

While everyone was waiting for His reply, He bent down and wrote something in the sand. Then He stood up and said, "Let any one of you who is without sin be the first to throw a stone at her" (verse 7, NIV).

One by one, the people walked away. They had their own sins to deal with.

Only Jesus and the woman remained. Jesus could have stoned her because He was "without sin" (verse 7; see also Hebrews 4:15). Instead, He said, "Where are your accusers? Didn't even one of them condemn you? ... Neither do I. Go and sin no more" (John 8:10–11).

Always default to love, and never throw stones. Let Jesus deal with the sin.

Don't just tell your kids to love others; show them how to do it. Our kids need to see us love people who are different from us. They also need to see us love people we don't agree with. Trust me, we can model love without compromising our beliefs.

If we *only* teach our kids to love but never talk about a moral compass, they won't be able to discern right from wrong in a world where everything is accepted. When lines are blurred, our kids will be confused and easily swayed.

If we *only* teach our kids right from wrong but never teach love, we will raise bullies who are judgmental and hateful. That isn't a good representation of Jesus or the church.

We need an equal balance of love and truth so we're modeling a true, authentic faith that our kids will want to imitate.

9. Overcome Fear

I hope by now you can see how open communication helps keep our kids safe. The next two talking points are a little different from the previous ones that focused on creating a culture of conversation *with our kids*. Now we're going to focus on preparing *ourselves* for implementing this solution. These points are important because we're responsible for building this new culture of conversation.

First, let's talk about fear. I realize that some of you may still feel overwhelmed and stuck in fear because all you can see is that big scary problem we discussed earlier: technology is exposing our kids to danger and changing how they're growing up.

Old Mandy was stuck there too. I was in shock as my own kids started to really open up about what they were being exposed to. The horrific stories other families shared with me caused so much fear and anxiety, I never wanted my kids to leave the house. I had a difficult time sleeping, and I'd often wake up in the middle of the night terrified over all of the issues parents have to handle today.

After seven years of creating this new culture in my home, though, New Mandy sleeps great (unless I'm traveling and sleeping in a hotel!). Want to know why?

No matter what my kids are exposed to online or what they hear from friends, I know they'll come home and ask me.

Fear of the unknown is gone!

I don't worry about what they're being exposed to, because I'm their safe place, their source of information. I know they'll confide in me. And because my kids trust me, I'm able to point them to the One who will never lead them down the wrong path: Jesus.

I still have concerns, and I hate what my kids have to deal with, but I'm not anxious or fearful anymore about what the world is going to throw at them. I don't spend all of my energy worrying about ways to make all the bad content go away. Instead, we just talk about what they see and hear. This has been so freeing!

It's natural to feel afraid (and even angry) because we can't control what the world throws at our babies. We have to acknowledge the emotions, but we can't allow ourselves to get stuck there. We must move on to the solution that *is* within our control: having healthy everyday conversations with our kids about what they're encountering.

This is how we keep them safe. What we're willing to talk about *today* will affect tomorrow. We change the world through our kids. When we know they're prepared for what they're walking into and have their own moral compass to rely on, the fear fades.

Above all, remember what God says to us in Isaiah 41:10: "Don't be afraid, for I am with you. Don't be discouraged for I am your God. I will strengthen you and help you."

That's a promise we can count on. No matter what happens in this world, God is with us, and He is able to use it for good. Deuteronomy 23:5 even says that He turns curses into blessings because He loves us.

Never in a million years would I have thought I'd say, "Our child being exposed to porn at the age of nine was one of the best things that has ever happened to us." But here I am.

God is turning curses into blessings! I'm seeing this happen as I travel to nextTalk events around the country. An awakening is happening in private and public schools, in the homeschool community, and in churches across all denominations. People are uniting to save our drowning children. We're engaging in a healthy dialogue about the difficult issues our children face. We're getting back to the basics and talking about the tough stuff.

Cyberparenting has blindsided all of us. It feels like we're caught in a storm, trying to keep our heads above water. But God hasn't been blindsided by any of this.

When the disciples were caught in a boat in the middle of a storm, Jesus told them, "Don't be afraid.... Take courage. I am here!" (Matthew 14:27). He says the same thing to us in the middle of the storms we face.

He knows what we're up against, and He's provided the solution.

10. Look in the Mirror

We've covered some tough subjects, but I've saved the most difficult talking point for last. Don't hate me! I wanted you to see the benefits of open communication before sharing where we need to start in creating this new culture. Brace yourself. This is going to sting!

Let's go back to the beginning of this story when my daughter was nine. I had finally defined the problem technology has caused for kids today, and I had discovered the solution. But I wasn't sure where to begin implementing it. *What's the next step?* I wondered.

Do you remember what Deuteronomy 6:7 says about talking to your kids when you're going to bed?

Well, one night as I tucked my child into bed, I felt prompted to crawl in next to her and ask, "How can I be a better mom?"

Her answer hurt me deeply.

She said, "Mom, you're not a good listener."

I immediately got defensive and thought, *Do you realize what I have to deal with every day? You have no clue how much I do for you!*

But I was trying really hard to be a good listener, so I bit my tongue.

Once I had gathered my thoughts, I said, "Can you give me an example?" (This is a great question to ask in any situation because it allows you to gather more information and context.)

Her reply was brutally honest: "Many times when I'm talking, you're on your phone, unloading the dishwasher, or cooking dinner. It makes me mad when I have to repeat my story because you weren't listening."

Ouch.

I lay there in her bed, in complete silence, feeling as if I had been punched in the gut. I didn't know how to respond. The sting I felt in that moment made me realize the solution started with me. That was the first time I realized Old Mandy needed to change.

Fighting back tears, I swallowed my pride and said, "I'm so sorry, sweetie. I'm juggling a lot, but you are more important than my job, Facebook, dinner, or anything else. You're right. I need to be a better listener. Will you help me? If I come back to you in a couple weeks, will you tell me how I'm doing?"

And she did! One time she even gave me a report card with heart stickers. Now that she's older, her feedback looks way different, but I still regularly ask her, "How am I doing? How can I be a better mom in this season of your life?" For my birthday this year, she gave me the sweetest handwritten card that said, "You've gotten a lot better at listening." Best present ever!

My daughter's feedback showed me what I wasn't getting right and what I needed to do differently. She needed to be heard, and I needed to look in the mirror. My daughter has helped me become New Mandy.

We can't create meaningful conversation unless we learn to listen. We need to welcome real, honest feedback from our kids. It may sting, but if we let their words penetrate our hearts, shape our character, and improve our communication skills, it can transform our parenting.

When I set out on this journey, I was searching for a way to keep my kids safe online. That's what we all want, right? But creating a healthy culture of open communication has accomplished so much more than that. Little did I know that God would give me a solution that would impact every facet of my life!

I've been amazed at how open communication has transformed my marriage. Old Mandy didn't even know I had a bad marriage!

And you wouldn't believe the conversations my husband is having with our kids now. He used to be reluctant to talk with them, but not anymore.

One morning he took the kids to school because I had an important meeting. Just as I was walking into the office building, he called me and said with uncharacteristic enthusiasm, "It works! It works!"

My husband does not get worked up. Ever.

I whispered into the phone, "Babe, what are you talking about?"

"Open communication," he replied with loud excitement. "It really works! I just had ten minutes in the car with the kids, and we talked pornography and masturbation."

By this time, I was inside the quiet office building. I looked around to make sure no one heard him say those words! (So embarrassed.)

Y'all, this was *after* my first book came out! It took my husband a little while to get on board, but it's been beautiful to watch him find his own rhythm of talking with our kids.

My children have changed too!

One morning on the drive to school, one of my kids had attitude. I knew why. This child was stressed about a certain class. But New Mandy stayed calm and didn't snap back.

After exiting the car and walking toward the school building, my teen stopped and then came back to say, "I'm sorry, Mom. I had attitude. I was stressed. I don't want to start my day like that."

I teared up! My kids have seen me humbly admit my own faults and apologize to them. And now they're imitating the behavior I've modeled. They've seen me working on my own faults, and now they come to me and say, "I think I need to work on this, Mom."

I'm in awe of God's wisdom!

One of the most important lessons I've learned is that change begins with me. As parents, we don't mean to shut down communication in our homes, but we often do. When your child tries to talk with you, are you a poor listener like me? Do you respond in anger or sweep topics under the rug because you don't know what to say? Do you have baggage from the past that prevents you from talking about an issue?

If we want open, honest communication with our kids, we need to look in the mirror and work on our own blind spots. I know that hurts, but it's true.

Here's something else my best friend tells me: When you look in the mirror and see your flaws (we all have them), a perfect Jesus is staring back at you, and He loves you *just as you are*. If you let

Him guide you, He'll transform you. And that will change the culture of your home.

We can't teach our kids to seek Jesus if we aren't seeking Him. We can't expect them to be emotionally healthy and balanced with screens if we aren't. We can't get upset when our kids become confused about boundaries if we haven't helped them develop a moral compass. And we can't prepare them for life or teach them to safely navigate their online world if we're frozen in fear.

But there is hope! As we build a new culture of conversation with our kids, we'll find *ourselves* changing along the way. We'll become better parents and people.

When I started this process, I didn't know where to begin or what to say, but I had a willing heart. I was ready to be molded and taught. So I asked God to show me, and look what He's done. I'm still amazed!

If you're not sure where to begin or what to say, let God show you. Crawl in bed tonight with your child and ask, "How can I be a better parent?" Be ready for the sting and don't get defensive. Maybe you can start with an apology. God will guide you every step of the way. Pray for words and wisdom. You can trust Him.

My prayer is that your children will start opening up to you as you focus on building open communication in your home. You're going to be shocked at what their little minds are worrying about.

Have the courage to look in the mirror and make the changes you need to make so you can lead the conversations with your kids and implement these ten ideas.

My hope is that when you go to bed at night, you'll find yourself saying, "I rocked that today!" I'd love for you to see the tide begin to turn in your family as you create a culture of healthy, ongoing conversations with your kids.

Technology is changing the way our kids are growing up. It's exposing them to new dangers, but as nextTalk families, we're learning how to keep our kids safe and prepare them for life. We've found a solution that works, and it starts with us.

So let's rise to the challenge, parents. We can do this!

NOTES

1. Victoria L. Dunckley, "Will Your Gamer Survive College?" *Mental Wealth* (blog), *Psychology Today*, September 26, 2016, www.psychologytoday.com/us/blog/mental-wealth/201609/ will-your-gamer-survive-college.

2. Richard Graham, cited in Victoria Ward, "Toddlers Becoming So Addicted to iPads They Require Therapy," *Telegraph*, April 21, 2013, www.telegraph.co.uk/technology/10008707/ Toddlers-becoming-so-addicted-to-iPads-they-require- therapy.html.

3. Josh McDowell Ministry and Barna Group, *The Porn Phenomenon: The Explosive Growth of Pornography and How It's Impacting Your Church, Life, and Ministry* (Plano, TX: Josh McDowell Ministry, 2016), cited in Chrissy Gordon, "Key Findings in Landmark Pornography Study Released," Josh

McDowell Ministry, January 19, 2016, www.josh.org/key-findings-in-landmark-pornography-study-released/. Used by permission.

4. "The 2019 Year in Review," Pornhub Insights, December 11, 2019, https://www.pornhub.com/insights/2019-year-in-review.

5. Mayo Clinic staff, "Self-Injury/Cutting: Symptoms and Causes," 1996–2020, https://www.mayoclinic.org/diseases-conditions/self-injury/symptoms-causes/syc-20350950.

6. Sameer Hinduja and Justin W. Patchin, "Bullying, Cyberbullying, and Suicide," *Archives of Suicide Research* 14, no. 3 (2010), cited in David D. Luxton, Jennifer D. June, and Jonathan M. Fairall, "Social Media and Suicide: A Public Health Perspective," *American Journal of Public Health* 102, supp. 2 (May 2012), www.ncbi.nlm.nih.gov/pmc/articles/PMC3477910/.

7. Melonie Heron, "Deaths: Leading Causes for 2017," *National Vital Statistics Reports* 68, no. 6 (June 2019): 17, www.cdc.gov/nchs/data/nvsr/nvsr68/nvsr68_06-508.pdf.

8. Dean G. Kilpatrick, Benjamin E. Saunders, and Daniel W. Smith, *Youth Victimization: Prevalence and Implications* (Washington, DC: US Department of Justice, 2003), 5, www.ncjrs.gov/pdffiles1/nij/194972.pdf.

9. "American Academy of Pediatrics Supports Childhood Sleep Guidelines," American Academy of Pediatrics, June 13, 2016, www.aap.org/en-us/about-the-aap/aap-press-room/Pages/American-Academy-of-Pediatrics-Supports-Childhood-Sleep-Guidelines.aspx.

RECOMMENDED RESOURCES

Books

Jenson, Kristen A. *Good Pictures, Bad Pictures Jr.* Richland, WA: Glen Cove Press, 2017.

Jenson, Kristen A., and Gail Poyner. *Good Pictures, Bad Pictures: Porn-Proofing Today's Young Kids.* Richland, WA: Glen Cove Press, 2016.

Majors, Mandy. *TALK: A Practical Approach to Cyberparenting and Open Communication.* Self-published, 2017.

Perry, Jackie Hill. *Gay Girl, Good God: The Story of Who I Was and Who God Has Always Been.* Nashville: B&H Publishing Group, 2018.

Organizations and Websites

Bark—bark.us. A research-driven, kid-friendly web monitoring and filtering service that helps parents keep their children safe online. The service not only monitors the most popular social media platforms and apps, but it also provides alerts, screen-time management, and web-filtering tools.

David's Legacy Foundation—davidslegacy.org. A nonprofit organization dedicated to protecting children from all forms of bullying through advocacy, education, legislation, and legal action.

Fight the New Drug—fightthenewdrug.org. A nonprofit organization that uses science-based facts, school presentations, blog articles, and personal stories to increase awareness of pornography's destructive effects. The organization also offers an online program (Fortify) to help people recover from porn addiction.

National Center on Sexual Exploitation—endsexualexploitation. org. A leading national organization that exposes the connection between pornography, sex trafficking, and other forms of sexual exploitation; educates the public; and fights sexual exploitation through legal and policy channels.

National Suicide Prevention Lifeline—suicidepreventionlifeline. org; 800-273-8255. A network of crisis centers that provide 24/7 crisis and suicide-prevention services, resources, and support.

nextTalk—nexttalk.org. A nonprofit organization that helps parents keep kids safe online by creating a culture of honest conversation at home. In addition to hosting parenting conferences, the nextTalk team speaks at church and school events and offers a variety of resources for parents, including podcasts and video studies. Follow nextTalk on Facebook, Instagram, and Twitter.

Plugged In—pluggedin.com. An entertainment guide that publishes reviews of movies, TV programs, books, music, video games, and other kinds of entertainment. Provides invaluable tools for understanding and navigating today's culture.

Protect Young Eyes—protectyoungeyes.com. A site that offers webinars, school presentations, app reviews, technology information, and other resources to help parents protect children from online danger.

Protect Young Minds—protectyoungminds.org. An organization led by the author of *Good Pictures, Bad Pictures* that informs, equips, and empowers parents and community leaders to protect kids from pornography and help them heal from sexual exploitation.

Proverbs 31 Ministries—proverbs31.org. A ministry that encourages women to seek a personal relationship with Jesus Christ and grow spiritually through radio messages, Bible studies, conferences, and other resources and events.

Made in the USA
Las Vegas, NV
19 January 2025

16498813R10059